ADRINA ELROD

Glow Up Your OnlyFans: The No-BS Guide to Going Viral, Making Bank, and Building a Loyal Fanbase

From Monetizing Content to Growing a Fanbase—All the Marketing, Legal, and Engagement Tips You Need

Copyright © 2024 by Adrina Elrod

All rights reserved. No part of this publication may be reproduced, stored or transmitted in any form or by any means, electronic, mechanical, photocopying, recording, scanning, or otherwise without written permission from the publisher. It is illegal to copy this book, post it to a website, or distribute it by any other means without permission.

Adrina Elrod asserts the moral right to be identified as the author of this work.

Adrina Elrod has no responsibility for the persistence or accuracy of URLs for external or third-party Internet Websites referred to in this publication and does not guarantee that any content on such Websites is, or will remain, accurate or appropriate.

Designations used by companies to distinguish their products are often claimed as trademarks. All brand names and product names used in this book and on its cover are trade names, service marks, trademarks and registered trademarks of their respective owners. The publishers and the book are not associated with any product or vendor mentioned in this book. None of the companies referenced within the book have endorsed the book.

First edition

This book was professionally typeset on Reedsy.
Find out more at reedsy.com

Contents

About The Book — v
Introduction — 1
The Scoop on OnlyFans — 2
    Control Over Content and Pricing — 2
    Privacy and Security Features — 2
    Why OnlyFans is Popular — 3
Ready to Make it Official? Setting Up Your OnlyFans — 4
    Account Setup and Verification — 4
    Building a Killer Profile — 4
    Setting Subscription Prices — 5
    Get to Know the Tools — 5
Content Creation: Time to Get Creative! — 6
    Optimized Content Ideas for OnlyFans — 6
    Quality over Quantity — 8
    Experiment with Different Content Types — 8
    Consistency is Key — 9
Special Tips for Adult Content Creators — 10
    1. Identify Your Niche and Embrace It — 10
    2. Quality Counts – Invest in Your Setup — 11
    3. Experiment with Different Content Types — 11
    4. Set Boundaries and Communicate Them Clearly — 11
    5. Engage with Fans, But Don't Overwhelm Yourself — 12
    6. Be Creative with Themes and Scenarios — 12
Getting Noticed: How to Promote Your OnlyFans — 13
    1. Social Media Is Your Friend – Use It Wisely — 13
    2. Collaborate with Other Creators for Exposure — 14

3. Run Exclusive Promotions to Create Urgency	14
4. Engage Creatively on Stories and Live Videos	14
5. Network in Niche Communities	15
6. Build an Email List to Stay in Touch	15
Keeping Things Running Smoothly	16
1. Create a Content Calendar and Stick to It	16
2. Use Analytics to Learn What Works	17
3. Set Subscriber Expectations Clearly	17
4. Handle Payments and Refunds Professionally	17
5. Keep Up with Platform Updates and New Features	18
6. Backup Your Content Regularly	18
Keeping Your Persona Consistent & Real	19
Be Real, Not a Character	19
Setting Boundaries While Staying Friendly	20
Use Your Tone and Style Consistently	20
Manage Your Privacy Smartly	21
Legal Know-How: What You Need to Know	22
Know the Platform's Terms of Service (TOS)	22
Protect Your Content from Being Stolen	23
Age Verification and Legal Documentation	23
Copyrights and Trademarks: Use Your Own Stuff	24
Stay Up-to-Date with Changing Policies	24
Etiquette and Best Practices to Build Trust	25
Be Responsive (But Don't Overwhelm Yourself)	25
Respect Fans' Boundaries Too	26
Keep It Professional, Even When Handling Negative Feedback	26
Engage Creatively with Your Community	26
Stick to Your Content Plan	27
Maintain Your Reputation as You Grow	27
Wrapping It Up: Your OnlyFans Journey Starts Now	28

About The Book

Heyyy, future content queen (or king!) 👑! Ready to **slay the OnlyFans game** and bag those 💰 **subs and $$** like a pro? Whether you're just dipping your toes or already flexing your creator muscles, this guide is your VIP pass to **OnlyFans stardom**. We're spilling all the tea on crafting a killer brand, making **fire content**, and growing a fanbase that's literally obsessed with you. Get ready to watch those subscribers hit that "Follow" button like it's their side hustle!

Why You'll Love This Book:

- **Ultimate How-To**: From setting up your account to **creating content that POPS**, we've got the 411 on everything.
- **Fanbase Growth Hacks**: Learn how to build a ride-or-die community that keeps coming back for more.
- **Marketing Like a Boss**: Master the art of promoting your page across **Instagram**, **TikTok**, and more. Get those eyeballs on your content!
- **Max Earning Tips**: We're talking **tiered subs**, pay-per-view magic, and even slinging your own merch! 💰
- **Stay Safe & Legal**: Keep it real with tips on privacy, security, and navigating the OnlyFans rules like a pro.

Perfect For:

- **Aspiring OnlyFans creators** looking to start strong and make bank 💵.
- **Experienced pros** who want to level up their game and **maximize earnings**.

- Creators of all kinds—whether you're into fitness, lifestyle, spicy content (👀), or something totally unique, this book's got you covered.

If you're ready to **turn your creative passion** into a full-time hustle, this guide is your new BFF. Let's get those coins, build that fanbase, and have fun doing it. **Your OnlyFans glow-up starts now**—let's gooo!

Introduction

Hey, future OnlyFans superstar! Ready to kick off your digital content journey? Whether you're a seasoned pro looking to flex your skills or a total newbie ready to dive in, this guide is your ultimate playbook for OnlyFans success. We're talking all the tea on building a loyal fanbase, creating fire content, and marketing yourself like a boss. Let's get those subscribers hitting that "Subscribe" button and watch your income skyrocket!

The Scoop on OnlyFans

OnlyFans is a powerful subscription-based platform that lets creators make real money by sharing exclusive content with a loyal fanbase. Although it's best known for adult content, it's used by creators across all industries, from fitness trainers to artists. However, it's definitely a favorite for adult content creators looking to monetize their unique skills.

Control Over Content and Pricing

On OnlyFans, you're in control of what you share and how much fans pay to access it. Some creators keep certain content free, while others add exclusive, premium tiers for VIP fans willing to pay extra. You set your membership rates, creating a personalized OnlyFans experience that reflects your brand.

Privacy and Security Features

OnlyFans has privacy and security features specifically designed to help creators protect their content and stay safe online. This is especially important for adult content creators. Options like user-blocking, search engine privacy settings, and age verification keep both creators and subscribers safe on the platform.

Why OnlyFans is Popular

Creators love OnlyFans because it allows for direct audience interaction and provides a steady income stream while they keep creative control. However, OnlyFans does come with its own set of rules and legal standards, so a clear understanding of the platform's requirements will make your experience smooth and successful.

Ready to Make it Official? Setting Up Your OnlyFans

Before you start posting, it's essential to get your OnlyFans account set up. Follow these steps to make sure your profile stands out.

Account Setup and Verification

To set up an account, OnlyFans will ask for basics like your name, birthdate, and payment info, plus age verification to ensure compliance (you must be over 18). This verification process ensures OnlyFans remains a safe space for both creators and fans.

Building a Killer Profile

The first thing potential subscribers see is your profile, so make it shine! Here are a few tips:

Profile Picture:
   Choose a high-quality image that represents your brand and the type of content you'll offer. If you're an adult content creator, pick an eye-catching

yet tasteful image that gives a hint at your style.

Bio:

Keep it short and catchy, making sure to tell visitors exactly what they can expect. Highlight your niche, the frequency of posts, and any exclusive perks.

Setting Subscription Prices

Pricing your OnlyFans content strategically makes a big difference. Browse other creators in your niche and see what rates are common, then set your prices to reflect the value you're offering. Experiment with different tiers to let fans choose the access level they want, whether it's exclusive content or one-on-one interactions.

Get to Know the Tools

OnlyFans has several tools to help you engage with fans, including DMs, tipping options, and live streams. Familiarize yourself with these features, as they're great for building relationships and creating opportunities to monetize in new ways. Watching your analytics is a great way to track your success and identify what types of posts your fans love most.

Content Creation: Time to Get Creative!

Creating content that's engaging, high-quality, and consistent is the secret to keeping your OnlyFans subscribers happy. Here's how to keep things fresh while maximizing engagement.

Optimized Content Ideas for OnlyFans

- **Behind-the-Scenes Content**:

Show followers the making of your content—prepping for a shoot, setting up lighting, or even casual day-in-the-life clips. Behind-the-scenes content builds a personal connection with fans, giving them a unique look into your world.

- **Q&A Sessions**:

Host live Q&As where fans can ask questions, or record pre-filmed Q&As from fan-submitted questions. These are great for building loyalty and making fans feel closer to you.

- **Exclusive Tutorials**:

Share tutorials that play to your strengths. Whether it's beauty routines, fitness tips, or something niche, tutorials make your account more valuable to fans looking to learn from you.

- **Personal Stories and Life Updates**:

Share occasional personal updates, like your goals or challenges. This adds a human touch to your profile, helping fans feel more connected to your journey.

- **Themed Content Days**:

Get creative with weekly themes, like "Fan Friday" or "Throwback Thursday." Themed days give fans something to look forward to and add fun variety to your posting schedule.

- **Interactive Polls and Votes**:

Engage fans by letting them vote on outfits, themes, or future content ideas. Polls are a great way to boost engagement and make fans feel involved.

- **VIP Exclusive Content**:

Offer top-tier fans special access to exclusive photos, videos, or live streams. VIP content rewards your loyal subscribers, encouraging them to stay subscribed longer.

- **Collaborations with Other Creators**:

Team up with other creators in your niche to create fresh content and expose your profile to new audiences. Collaborative content is fun and expands your fanbase.

- **Personalized Shoutouts and Messages**:

Consider offering personalized messages or birthday shoutouts. Personal interactions help build a more loyal fanbase and make subscribers feel appreciated.

- **Challenges and Series Content**:

Run a "30-Day Challenge" or a monthly series, giving fans something consistent to follow. This boosts engagement by creating anticipation for each new post.

Quality over Quantity

Focus on quality posts rather than flooding your page. Investing in good lighting and sound equipment makes a big difference, especially for fans willing to pay for premium content.

Experiment with Different Content Types

Try a mix of content—videos, photos, live streams, and audio clips to see what fans love most. Throw in personalized messages to keep things exciting and interactive.

Consistency is Key

A regular posting schedule keeps fans engaged and coming back for more. A content calendar can help you plan, track ideas, and make sure you're delivering consistently high-quality content.

Special Tips for Adult Content Creators

So, you're diving into adult content on OnlyFans? Amazing! Adult content can be super lucrative on OnlyFans, and fans love creators who know how to bring originality and value. But it also comes with some unique challenges and responsibilities. Here's how to stand out and stay safe in the adult content game while keeping fans engaged.

1. Identify Your Niche and Embrace It

"Adult content" is a broad category, so finding a specific niche can help you stand out. Are you all about solo content? Maybe you're into cosplay, fitness, or an edgy, alternative aesthetic? Discover what makes your content unique, and lean into it hard. This helps attract fans who are into exactly what you're offering, building a loyal following.

Example:
If you're into cosplay, make a series where you dress up as fan-favorite characters. Or, if fitness is your thing, create content that blends workout routines with playful and adult themes.

2. Quality Counts – Invest in Your Setup

Fans can tell the difference between high-quality and thrown-together content, and they're willing to pay for a premium experience. Investing in good lighting, a quality camera, and maybe even a ring light can make all the difference. Your fans will appreciate the effort, and you'll look pro-level from the get-go.

Tip:
If you're on a budget, start with a smartphone camera and inexpensive lighting setup. Later, you can upgrade as your income grows!

3. Experiment with Different Content Types

Keep things fresh by mixing up your content formats. While photos and videos are classics, you could try adding live streams, personalized audio clips, or even animated gifs. Fans love variety, and trying new formats can help you discover what types of content get the most engagement.

Pro Tip:
Host a live Q&A or do a poll asking fans what kind of content they'd love to see more of. This keeps your fans engaged and gives you ideas for future posts.

4. Set Boundaries and Communicate Them Clearly

Being an adult content creator can blur lines between the personal and professional, so it's essential to set boundaries. Communicate openly with fans about what's on the table and what's off-limits. This keeps interactions respectful and prevents uncomfortable situations.

Example:
If you're open to DMs but prefer no personal questions, put this in your bio or make it part of a welcome message to new subscribers.

5. Engage with Fans, But Don't Overwhelm Yourself

Adult content fans often appreciate one-on-one interactions, but it's okay to manage your time. Set boundaries on when and how you respond to messages. It's great to be friendly and engaging but keep it sustainable to avoid burnout.

Tip:
Use OnlyFans' features to create short video or voice replies to common questions. This saves time and keeps fans engaged without requiring constant one-on-one communication.

6. Be Creative with Themes and Scenarios

Adult content can quickly get repetitive, so try experimenting with themes, settings, and scenarios. Try dressing up for special events (like a Halloween series) or creating fun, themed photo sets. Creativity keeps fans excited and encourages them to renew their subscriptions.

Hack:
Plan a "Fan Friday" theme, where fans can choose the look or scenario you'll create next. Fans love feeling involved, and it helps break up your usual content flow.

Getting Noticed: How to Promote Your OnlyFans

Creating amazing content is just the first step. The next big move is getting that content in front of people who will pay to see it. Promotion on OnlyFans is all about using social media, networking with other creators, and building your brand online. Here's the play-by-play to attract new subscribers and keep them coming back.

1. Social Media Is Your Friend – Use It Wisely

Platforms like Instagram, Twitter, and TikTok are incredible tools for promoting your OnlyFans, but each has different rules. Instagram is more visual and may have restrictions on adult content, while Twitter is a bit more lenient. Tailor your posts to each platform and use hashtags to reach a wider audience.

Tip:
   Use Linktree or another link-in-bio service to centralize all your social media links and your OnlyFans profile. This makes it easy for fans to find all your platforms from a single link.

2. Collaborate with Other Creators for Exposure

Collaborations are one of the best ways to grow your fanbase. By teaming up with creators who share your niche or have a similar vibe, you'll gain access to their followers, and they'll gain access to yours. This can be as simple as a shoutout or as involved as a co-created piece of content.

Example:
   Run a "guest feature" where you swap shoutouts with another creator. Or, plan a joint live stream Q&A with a creator whose audience complements yours.

3. Run Exclusive Promotions to Create Urgency

Everybody loves a good discount! Consider running limited-time promotions or offering exclusive discounts to new subscribers. These incentives create urgency, motivating potential subscribers to sign up right away.

Hack:
   Plan a "Flash Sale Friday" once a month where new fans get a discount. Regular promotions create anticipation and give you a consistent way to attract new followers.

4. Engage Creatively on Stories and Live Videos

Social media stories and live videos are perfect for giving fans a sneak peek of your content without sharing everything. Use these platforms to preview your OnlyFans, talk about your latest posts, or let fans ask questions. It's a low-effort way to stay in your followers' minds and spark interest.

Tip:
Go live once a week to answer questions, chat with fans, or just talk about what's new. Live videos can boost engagement and keep fans excited about what's next.

5. Network in Niche Communities

Joining niche communities—whether it's a Twitter list or a Facebook group—can expand your reach beyond typical social media. These groups are often full of supportive creators who share tips, promote each other, and offer advice.

Pro Tip:
Some Reddit communities allow OnlyFans promotion. Search for subreddits related to your niche, but be mindful of each community's rules.

6. Build an Email List to Stay in Touch

An email list is one of the most underrated tools for promoting OnlyFans. Emails let you stay connected even if your social media gets flagged or restricted. Build your list by offering freebies or exclusive content in exchange for email sign-ups, and use it to announce new content or promotions.

Hack:
Offer a free photo or video preview in exchange for an email sign-up. Fans who subscribe to your email list are usually more loyal and engaged!

Keeping Things Running Smoothly

Keeping your OnlyFans account organized is key to sustainable growth and steady income. Running a successful page means managing your time, planning content in advance, and using tools to track your progress. Let's look at how to stay on top of everything without losing your chill.

1. Create a Content Calendar and Stick to It

A content calendar is a lifesaver. It helps you plan posts, schedule special events, and stay consistent. Consistency not only makes you look reliable but also keeps fans engaged because they know when to expect new content.

Example:
   Plan out a month's worth of content with specific themes or weekly series. You could do "Motivation Monday" posts one week and "Fan Friday" Q&A's the next.

2. Use Analytics to Learn What Works

OnlyFans provides stats that show you which content is getting the most engagement, likes, or comments. Use these insights to see what fans respond to best and adjust your strategy accordingly. Analytics help you learn what your fans enjoy, so you can give them more of it.

Pro Tip:
   Track things like peak engagement times, most-liked posts, and highest-earning days. This helps you plan future content for the best results.

3. Set Subscriber Expectations Clearly

Setting expectations helps you avoid misunderstandings and keeps fans happy. A clear description of what they'll get—like weekly posts, exclusive content for VIPs, or live streams—keeps them satisfied and less likely to unsubscribe.

Tip:
   Use a pinned welcome message or an introductory post for new fans. Outline your posting schedule, content types, and anything else they should know about your page.

4. Handle Payments and Refunds Professionally

OnlyFans takes care of payment processing, but keeping an eye on your earnings and any potential refunds is still a good habit. If a fan is unhappy or requests a refund, respond professionally to maintain a good reputation.

Example:

If a fan claims they didn't receive promised content, double-check and politely offer a resolution. Staying professional keeps things smooth.

5. Keep Up with Platform Updates and New Features

OnlyFans frequently updates its features and policies, so stay in the loop! New tools like pay-per-view messaging, video calls, or story features can open up new revenue streams. Keep up with updates so you can make the most out of the platform.

Hack:

Set a monthly reminder to check OnlyFans updates or blog posts. Staying informed gives you an edge and helps you use the platform more effectively.

6. Backup Your Content Regularly

It's always smart to have backups of your work. In case of any platform glitches or if you decide to move to another site, having a backup means you won't lose any content. Use a secure cloud service or an external hard drive to save copies of everything.

Tip:

Every week or month, take 15 minutes to back up your latest posts. This keeps your content safe and gives you peace of mind.

Keeping Your Persona Consistent & Real

Alright, so here's the thing—on OnlyFans, *you* are the brand, and fans are following you because they vibe with who you are. But with that comes the responsibility of maintaining a consistent online persona. Whether you're putting out spicy content, sharing lifestyle tips, or just keeping it real, creating a genuine connection is key to building a fanbase that sticks around. Let's dive into how to keep things authentic while boosting your brand.

Be Real, Not a Character

The best part about platforms like OnlyFans is that it's all about being you. Gone are the days of overly filtered, perfect personas; Gen Z is all about *authenticity*. So drop the script and give fans the real you. Share your quirks, be open about what excites you, and let your unique personality shine. Fans are looking for creators they can connect with—not just a picture-perfect facade.

Tip:
If you're having a bad day or you're just not feeling it, it's okay to let fans know! Posting a story or a quick update keeps things real and reminds fans you're human.

Setting Boundaries While Staying Friendly

Being approachable doesn't mean you have to cross personal boundaries. It's cool to share parts of your day or behind-the-scenes content, but draw a line where you need to. This keeps your private life separate while still allowing fans to feel like they're part of your world. It's all about creating that VIP access feeling without letting it get too personal.

Example:
   Maybe you share your daily skincare routine or your favorite playlist but keep details about your location, family, or relationships private.

Use Your Tone and Style Consistently

When fans visit your profile, they should instantly get a sense of who you are. Is your vibe more casual and funny? Or maybe you're a bit more bold and mysterious? Whatever your style, keep it consistent across all posts, captions, and messages. Think of it like an aesthetic—you want fans to recognize *your voice* no matter what content they're looking at.

Tip:
   Stick to a set of words or phrases that match your personality. If you're going for a light, playful tone, using emojis and fun expressions works. For a more chill vibe, keeping it minimal and straightforward could work better.

Manage Your Privacy Smartly

Protecting your privacy while being active on OnlyFans is like walking a tightrope—but it's doable. OnlyFans has features like blocking specific users or hiding your profile from search engines. Make full use of these tools to keep the personal stuff out of your professional OnlyFans career.

Tip:
Set up a stage name or OnlyFans-specific handle if you want extra privacy. This keeps your OnlyFans persona separate from your real identity.

Legal Know-How: What You Need to Know

No one likes the boring legal stuff, but trust me, it's way better than facing issues later on. OnlyFans has rules, and so does the internet as a whole. So before you dive too deep, let's get you set up with some essential knowledge that'll keep you compliant, safe, and worry-free.

Know the Platform's Terms of Service (TOS)

Think of the TOS as the "house rules." OnlyFans has specific guidelines about what content is allowed, what's restricted, and what could get you banned. From adult content restrictions to prohibitions against hate speech or unlicensed music, understanding the TOS is crucial.

Example:

For example, OnlyFans might have specific guidelines about sharing sensitive content or certain age restrictions. Know these limits so your account doesn't risk a strike or a ban.

Protect Your Content from Being Stolen

Your content is valuable—so protect it! Watermarking your images or videos is one way to prevent unauthorized sharing. If someone tries to share your work elsewhere, a watermark makes it harder for them to pass it off as their own. Also, if you notice your content floating around on other sites, you can file DMCA takedown notices to have it removed.

Tip:
Use OnlyFans' privacy settings to hide your profile from search engines or block specific users if needed.

Age Verification and Legal Documentation

OnlyFans requires all creators to verify their age to ensure everyone on the platform is legally able to post content. You might need to submit additional documentation as well, depending on your location or content type. Double-check local regulations too, since some places have stricter laws around adult content.

Pro Tip:
Keep a digital folder with all your legal documents—proof of age, any copyright registrations, and copies of TOS agreements—so everything's in one place if you need it.

Copyrights and Trademarks: Use Your Own Stuff

When it comes to OnlyFans, always use original or licensed content. Posting copyrighted music, logos, or images that you don't own can lead to serious trouble. For example, if you use a popular song in a video without permission, it could be flagged for copyright violation.

Hack:
   Stick to royalty-free music or background sounds in your videos. Sites like Epidemic Sound and YouTube Audio Library offer free-to-use music that's safe for all types of content.

Stay Up-to-Date with Changing Policies

Social platforms are always changing their policies, and OnlyFans is no exception. Regularly checking the platform's blog or updates page is a good habit so you're never caught off guard by new rules.

Tip:
   Set a calendar reminder to check for TOS updates every quarter. It's an easy way to stay compliant without constantly worrying about changing rules.

Etiquette and Best Practices to Build Trust

Building a successful OnlyFans profile isn't just about the content you post—it's also about how you interact with your fans and manage your brand. Maintaining a good reputation and keeping fans engaged is all about showing respect, keeping communication open, and handling everything like a pro.

Be Responsive (But Don't Overwhelm Yourself)

Fans love feeling seen and heard, but that doesn't mean you have to answer every message the second it arrives. Set aside specific times to respond to DMs or comments, and be mindful of what you promise. Over committing can lead to burnout, so keep responses friendly but set limits to protect your time.

Example:
   Let fans know upfront that you'll respond to DMs once a day or twice a week. This keeps them engaged while respecting your schedule.

Respect Fans' Boundaries Too

Fans appreciate creators who are friendly but professional. Avoid oversharing or getting too personal in a way that might make them uncomfortable. Keep interactions friendly and respectful, and if a fan crosses a line, it's okay to reinforce your boundaries politely.

Pro Tip:
You can set up automated welcome messages or polite responses for common questions. This keeps things professional without feeling too robotic.

Keep It Professional, Even When Handling Negative Feedback

Every creator faces criticism, and it's all about handling it like a champ. If someone leaves a negative comment or gives feedback, take a breath and respond professionally. Avoid getting defensive and, if the feedback is constructive, use it to make improvements.

Tip:
For trolls or rude comments, it's perfectly okay to ignore or block users. OnlyFans has options for muting or blocking individuals, which can help keep your space positive.

Engage Creatively with Your Community

Building a community is what sets top creators apart. Think of ways to make your fans feel included, like running polls or voting sessions on what content you should create next. You can even do shoutouts or host virtual meet-and-greets to make fans feel like VIPs.

Example:
Host a "Fan Appreciation Day" where you shout out a few loyal followers or answer their most-asked questions. Small gestures make a big impact!

Stick to Your Content Plan

Having a set content plan helps keep your brand consistent. Fans know what to expect and appreciate creators who stick to a schedule. Use tools like content calendars to stay organized and keep fans in the loop about upcoming posts, livestreams, or special events.

Hack:
Set up a pinned post that shows your content plan or weekly schedule. This keeps fans in the loop and lets them know when to expect new content.

Maintain Your Reputation as You Grow

As you gain more subscribers, your reputation becomes more important. Staying professional, being approachable, and keeping interactions respectful builds a positive image that fans will appreciate. A good reputation also attracts new fans and keeps your current followers loyal.

Pro Tip:
Every few months, ask your fans for feedback! It shows you care about their experience and can lead to new ideas for content that'll keep them excited to stick around.

Wrapping It Up: Your OnlyFans Journey Starts Now

Congrats! You're now equipped to launch a successful, engaging OnlyFans account. Success is all about finding your niche, staying authentic, and delivering valuable content. Remember to stay consistent, keep learning, and let your personality shine. Your OnlyFans journey is just beginning—go make it amazing!

Remember, this is a business so treat it as such.

www.ingramcontent.com/pod-product-compliance
Lightning Source LLC
Chambersburg PA
CBHW030044230526
45472CB00005B/1666